The Question & Answer Book

AMAZING MAGNETS

AMAZING MAGNETS

By David Adler
Illustrated by Dan Lawler

Troll Associates

Library of Congress Cataloging in Publication Data

Adler, David A.
    Amazing magnets.

    (The Question and answer book)
    Summary: Questions and answers provide basic informa-
tion about magnets and magnetism. Includes several
experiments.
        1. Magnets—Juvenile literature. [1. Magnets.
2. Questions and answers] I. Lawler, Dan, ill.   II. Title.
III. Series: Question and answer book (Troll Associates)
QC757.5.A34   1983   538′.2   82-17377
ISBN 0-89375-894-9
ISBN 0-89375-895-7 (pbk.)

Copyright © 1983 by Troll Associates, Mahwah, New Jersey

Printed in the United States of America
10   9   8   7   6   5   4   3   2   1

Have you ever held a magnet near a piece of metal?

If you have, you may have felt a strange pulling force. A magnet is attracted to certain metals. It pulls toward them. Once it touches the metal, the magnet holds on. When you try to pull the magnet away, you feel an invisible force holding the magnet and the metal together. That invisible force is called magnetism.

Who first discovered magnetism?

One story says that thousands of years ago a shepherd named Magnes stood on a certain black rock. When he tried to move, he felt something pulling at his sandals. The shepherd was standing on a magnetic rock called lodestone. The lodestone was pulling at the iron nails in his sandals. Some people say that magnets were named after Magnes the shepherd.

Other people say magnets were named after a place in Asia that was once called Magnesia. They say that large amounts of black lodestone rocks were found there.

When lodestone rocks were first discovered, the powers of magnetism were a mystery. People knew that some metals were attracted to the rocks, but they didn't know which ones. They also didn't know how to use the force of magnetism.

Today we know more about magnetism. We know which metals are attracted to a magnet. And we have found a great many uses for the force of magnetism.

Which metals will attract a magnet?

Magnets are attracted to anything made of iron, steel, nickel, or cobalt. A magnet will pull toward these metals and stick to them.

If you have a magnet, you can use it as a metal tester. But be careful with your magnet, and be careful with the metals you test. Don't hold your magnet too close to delicate instruments, such as watches. It could upset their movements.

First, place your magnet on a metal pot. If the magnet sticks to the pot, you know the pot is made from iron, steel, nickel, or cobalt. If the magnet doesn't stick, you know the pot is made from another metal, such as copper or brass or aluminum.

Try placing your magnet on the hood of a car. Does it stick? It should. Most cars are made from steel.

Your magnet shouldn't stick to a soda can. Most soda cans are made from aluminum. It should stick to a can of peas or tuna fish. Those cans are usually made from steel.

Try placing your magnet on a
penny. Does it stick? It shouldn't.
Pennies are made partly from copper.
Magnets are not attracted to copper.

Next, try placing your magnet on a nickel. Does it stick? If the coins we call "nickels" were made only from the metal called nickel, the magnet would stick easily. But "nickels" are made from a combination of metals. That's why the magnet doesn't stick.

Try these experiments.

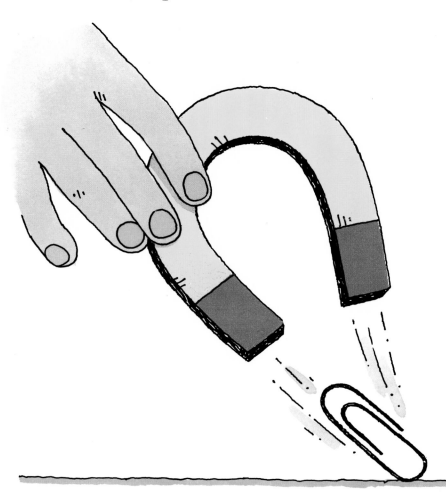

With a magnet and a paper clip, you can perform several experiments to find out about magnetism. Place the paper clip on a table. Hold your magnet a few inches above it. Slowly move the magnet closer. When the magnet comes close enough, the paper clip will jump through the air and attach itself to the magnet. That happens because the force of magnetism works through air.

Magnets also work through water, cloth, glass, and paper.

You can prove that the force of magnetism works through water. First, drop a paper clip into a bowl of water. Then place your magnet in the bowl. The paper clip should stick to the magnet.

You can also test your magnet to prove that it works through cloth. Cover a paper clip with a handkerchief. You should find that the force of magnetism attracts the paper clip to the magnet even though the handkerchief is in the way. The same thing will happen if glass or paper are placed between the paper clip and the magnet.

Here's a "magic" magnet:

Now that you know a magnet works through paper, you can make it do a magic trick. Draw a curved line on a sheet of paper. Place a paper clip on one end of the line. Hold the magnet against the other side of the paper, directly under the paper clip. Don't let your friends see the magnet. Tell them that without touching the paper clip, you can make it move along the curved line. It seems impossible, but with your hidden magnet, it's easy. Just move the magnet, and the paper clip will move along with it.

Since magnets work through paper, you can perform an experiment to find out more about the mysterious force of magnetism.

First, rub a file against an iron nail. Catch the metal filings on a sheet of paper. Then place the paper over a bar magnet. Tap the paper gently. The filings should now be arranged in a pattern. The pattern shows the "lines of force" around the magnet. These lines of force show the area of magnetic force that surrounds the magnet. This area is called a *magnetic field.*

The pattern of metal filings also shows the strength of the magnetic force. Where there are few metal filings, the force is weak. Where there are more filings, the force is stronger. You should find that the magnetic force is strongest at the ends of the magnet.

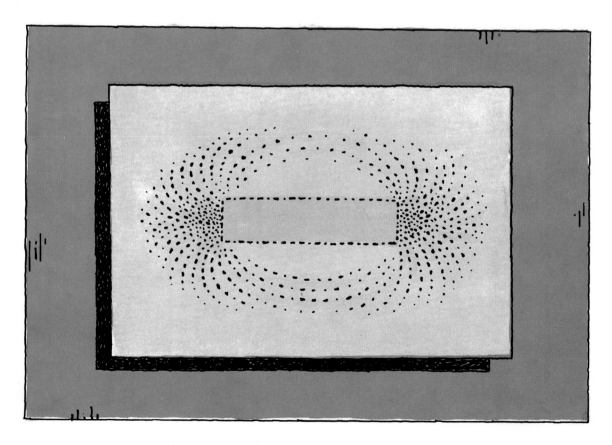

The ends of a magnet are called the poles. One end is called the north-seeking pole, or north pole. The other end is called the south-seeking pole, or south pole.

Are the two poles of a magnet different?

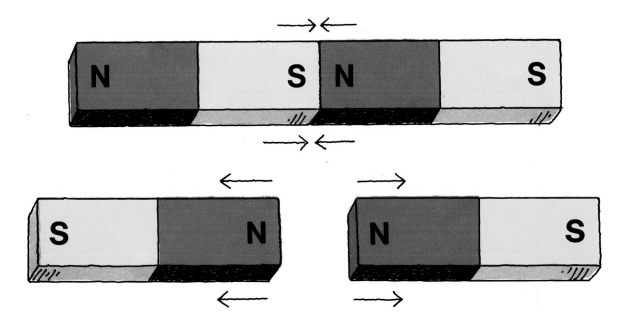

Yes. With two magnets you can prove it. Bring the magnets together so that one pole of each is touching. If the magnets stick together, you know the poles you brought together are different. One is a south-seeking pole. The other is a north-seeking pole. Opposite poles attract and stick together.

If the poles push away from each other, you know both are the same. Both are either north-seeking or south-seeking poles. Like poles repel each other.

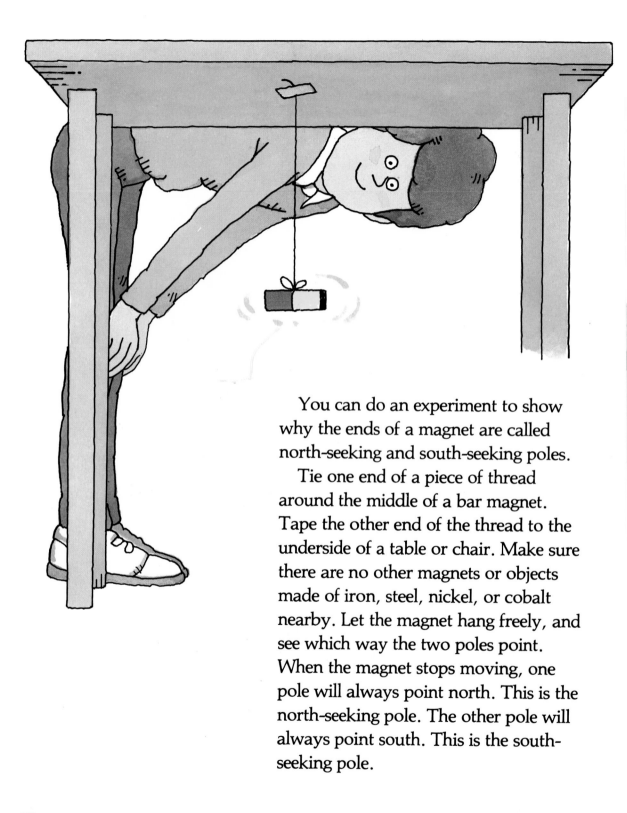

You can do an experiment to show why the ends of a magnet are called north-seeking and south-seeking poles.

Tie one end of a piece of thread around the middle of a bar magnet. Tape the other end of the thread to the underside of a table or chair. Make sure there are no other magnets or objects made of iron, steel, nickel, or cobalt nearby. Let the magnet hang freely, and see which way the two poles point. When the magnet stops moving, one pole will always point north. This is the north-seeking pole. The other pole will always point south. This is the south-seeking pole.

Hundreds of years ago, sailors discovered that one end of a magnet always points north. Since then, they have used magnets to make compasses. The needle in a compass is really a magnet. By pointing to the north, the needle has helped sailors, pilots, and explorers find their way.

One end of the compass needle always points north because the Earth itself is a large magnet. When the compass needle points north, the north-seeking pole of the compass magnet is really being drawn to the Earth's magnetic north pole, which is in the Arctic section of Canada. The south-seeking pole of the compass needle is drawn to the Earth's south magnetic pole, which is in Antarctica.

The first compasses sailors used were magnets floating freely on a piece of wood in a bowl of water. You can make a compass like theirs.

Here's how to make a compass.

Take a needle. Rub half the needle with one pole of a strong magnet. You should rub from the middle of the needle out toward the point. Keep using the same pole of the magnet and always rub in the same direction. After you have rubbed the needle about twenty times, it will become a magnet.

Tape the needle to a very small piece of cardboard. Place it in a bowl filled with water and allow it to float. When the needle stops moving, one end should be pointing north. For a while, every time you place it in the water the needle will point in the same direction. But the needle will not hold its magnetic powers forever. When you see that the needle no longer points north, rub it again with the same pole of the magnet.

Needles are made of steel. Steel can be magnetized. So can iron, nickel, and cobalt. The magnets we use today are made from those metals. They are called *artificial magnets*. Lodestone rocks are called *natural magnets* because they are found in nature.

Why can only certain metals be made into magnets?

And why are only certain metals attracted to magnets? All metals are made up of molecules, particles that are too small to see. Scientists believe the molecules that make up iron, steel, nickel, and cobalt are really tiny magnets.

Before the steel needle was made into a magnet, all its molecules were jumbled. Their north-seeking and south-seeking poles were pointing in many different directions.

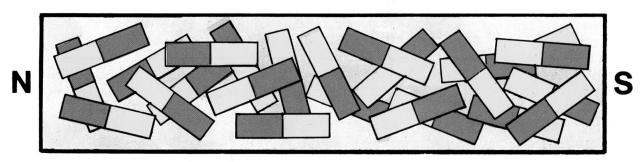

UNMAGNETIZED IRON BAR

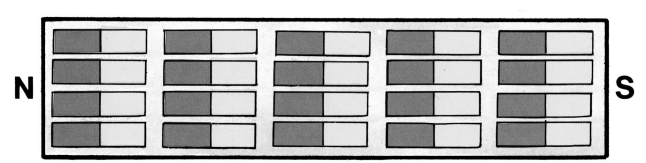

MAGNETIZED IRON BAR

When the needle was rubbed with a magnet, the tiny magnets inside became lined up, so that all the north-seeking poles faced in one direction, and all the south-seeking poles faced in the opposite direction. With all those tiny magnets facing the same way and working together, the needle became one large magnet.

Scientists have done an experiment to prove the theory that molecules of certain metals are really tiny magnets. They have broken a magnet in half. They found that each half became a complete magnet with a north-seeking pole and a south-seeking pole. They have broken the halves into smaller and smaller pieces. Each piece, no matter how small, was a complete magnet. Scientists believe that if they broke a magnet into the tiny molecules that make it up, each molecule would be a complete magnet.

Can a magnet lose its power?

You have seen that it is possible to line up the molecules in a needle and give it magnetic power. It is also possible to shake up the molecules in a magnet and make it lose its power.

If a magnet is dropped, hit hard with a hammer, or left in a very hot place, it loses some of its power. This is because the molecules in the magnet are shaken about and are moved out of line.

The best way to keep a magnet powerful is to store it away from heat and to cover its poles with a piece of iron.

Magnets are made in all different shapes. Many toy magnets are made in the shape of a horseshoe. But magnets used in computers are shaped like doughnuts. Radios and televisions use magnets shaped like coins. Magnets are also made into the shape of cylinders and long, rectangular bars.

27

Can you find the "hidden" magnets?

If you look around your house, you will probably find many magnets of different shapes at work.

A good place to start looking is in the kitchen. Often, magnets are hidden inside a strip of rubber on the inside of a refrigerator door. When the door is closed, the magnets pull the rubber up against the rest of the refrigerator. This seals the cold air inside. If you can make a paper clip stick to the strip of rubber in your refrigerator, there is a magnet inside.

Sometimes pairs of magnets keep cabinet doors closed. One magnet is fastened to the cabinet, and another is fastened to the door. They pull toward each other to keep the door closed.

28

Is there an electric can opener in your home? If there is, you will probably find a round magnet attached to it. The tops of cans are made from steel. The magnet holds on to them. Once the can is open, the magnet keeps the top from falling in.

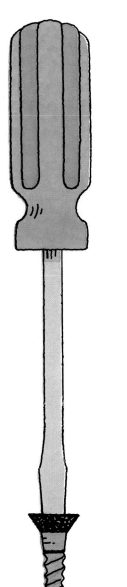

You might even find a magnet in your family tool chest. Sometimes screwdrivers are magnetized. This makes it easier to drive small screws into hard-to-get-at places. The magnetized tip of the screwdriver holds the screw, so you don't have to.

Is there a magnet in your family sewing kit? A magnet can save lots of time when someone has to pick up pins and needles that have dropped to the floor. That's why tailors usually have magnets handy.

You can't see them, but there are magnets inside your radio and television set. These magnets are very different from other magnets. Some people call them "on-off" magnets. They are also called *electromagnets.*

What is an electromagnet?

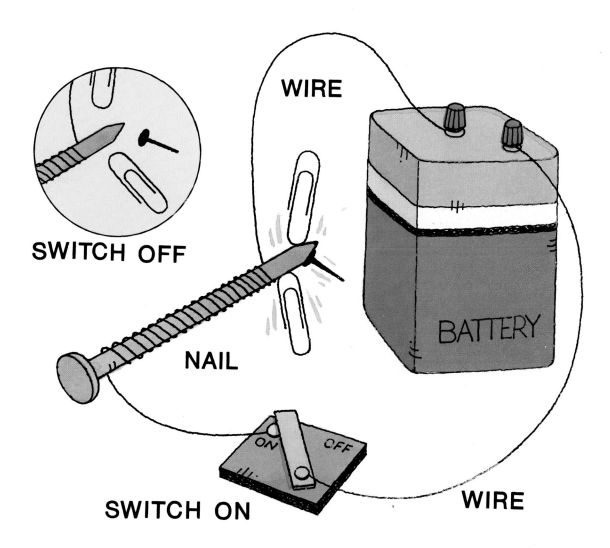

SWITCH OFF

WIRE

NAIL

SWITCH ON

BATTERY

WIRE

When electricity passes through wires, a magnetic field forms around the wires. Electromagnets are made by wrapping wires around a piece of metal. When electricity passes through the wires, the electromagnet has power. When the electricity is turned off, the electromagnet loses its power. Electromagnets are used in telephones, washing machines, and other electrical appliances.

Today magnets are used in a great many different ways. But scientists are continually looking for new ways to put magnets to work.

Scientists are also trying to learn more about how magnetism works, and why it works. Thousands of years have passed since Magnes the shepherd felt a strange force pulling at the nails in his sandals. But even today, there are still unanswered questions about the mysterious and fascinating force of magnetism.